EP Language Arts 6
Workbook

This book belongs to:

Luke David Williams

EP Language Arts 6 Workbook

ISBN-13: 978-1721227167
ISBN-10: 1721227164

First Edition: August, 2018

About this Workbook

This is an offline workbook for Easy Peasy All-in-One Homeschool's Language Arts 6 course. We've modified and expanded upon the online activities and printable worksheets available at the Easy Peasy All-in-One Homeschool website (www.allinonehomeschool.com) so that your child can work offline if desired. Whether you use the online or offline versions, or a combination of both, your child will enjoy these supplements to the Easy Peasy Language Arts course.

How to use this Workbook

This workbook is designed to be used in conjunction with Easy Peasy's Language Arts 6 Lesson Guide. As you and your child proceed through the Lesson Guide, use this workbook to exercise your child's language arts skills.

This workbook follows the EP online Language Arts course in sequential order, providing activity worksheets which can replace online activities and printable worksheets. However, this workbook does not include activity worksheets for the longer writing assignments. As such, this book does not contain 180 days of worksheets. The Lesson Guide will contain all writing assignments to make the course complete. There is also a brief description of them on the completion chart pages that follow (grayed out boxes denote no worksheet). If possible, allow your child to do these writing assignments on the computer to get practice typing and formatting papers.

The activity worksheets are designed with the following guidelines in mind:

- ## To supplement daily lessons
  This workbook on its own supplements, but does not replace, EP's daily lessons. Be sure to check the daily lesson on the website or in the Lesson Guide before having your child do the workbook activities.

- ## To serve as an alternative to online activities
  This workbook serves as an alternative to the activities posted online, providing offline activities in sufficient quantities and varieties to challenge your child. When used in conjunction with the Lesson Guide, this workbook becomes a complete offline course.

Please note, in the various places where nouns, verbs, adjectives, and adverbs are practiced, certain words can be categorized in more than one place (you can go for a swim [noun] or you can swim [verb]). If your child marks one of them differently than the answer key indicates, have a conversation with them to find out why.

- The solutions are on the website as well as in the Lesson Guide and are **not included** in this workbook.

Completion Chart for Lessons 1 - 45

1	following directions	16	writing	31	writing - commas
2	grammar/spelling	17	writing - simile/metaphor	32	writing - opinion about a book scene
3	syllables/spelling	18	verbs	33	commas
4	grammar/spelling	19	spelling	34	writing - copying sentence types
5	writing - ABAAB poem	20	similes	35	writing - setting
6	grammar	21	writing - metaphors	36	sentence types/ commas
7	writing - short story	22	writing - metaphors	37	writing - history
8	grammar	23	proofreading	38	spelling
9	grammar	24	proofreading	39	combining sentences
10	better sentences	25	grammar/spelling plurals	40	commas
11	metaphors	26	grammar/spelling plurals	41	spelling
12	writing - metaphors	27	writing - imaginary country	42	combining sentences
13	spelling	28	spelling	43	writing - sentence types
14	sentence fragments/ proofreading	29	writing - dialogue	44	independent clauses
15	similes	30	writing - dialogue	45	writing - book poster

*Grayed out boxes denote writing assignments that don't have a corresponding worksheet in this book.
Full writing assignments can be found online or in the Lesson Guide*

Completion Chart for Lessons 46 - 90

(46)	writing - book poster	(61)	writing - historical essay	(76)	types of advertising
(47)	writing - book poster	(62)	writing - historical essay	(77)	writing - advertisement
(48)	writing - book poster	(63)	writing - historical essay	(78)	advertisements
(49)	writing - book poster	(64)	editing - historical essay	(79)	compare/contrast advertisements
(50)	speaking - book poster	(65)	writing - letter	(80)	writing - advertisement
(51)	dialogue/writing - historical essay	(66)	proofreading	(81)	writing - funny story
(52)	dialogue/writing - historical essay	(67)	parts of speech	(82)	writing/parts of speech
(53)	writing/capitalization	(68)	writing - book report	(83)	writing - funny story
(54)	writing - historical essay	(69)	writing - book report	(84)	writing/parts of speech
(55)	commas/writing - historical essay	(70)	writing - book report	(85)	writing - funny story
(56)	writing - historical essay	(71)	editing - book report	(86)	writing - description
(57)	commas/writing - historical essay	(72)	adjectives	(87)	homophones
(58)	writing - historical essay	(73)	writing - letter	(88)	subject and object pronouns
(59)	sentence types	(74)	adjectives	(89)	pronouns
(60)	writing - advertisement	(75)	writing - letter	(90)	pronouns

Completion Chart for Lessons 91-135

(91)	proofreading	(106)	writing/spelling	(121)	adverbs and adjectives
(92)	semicolons	(107)	writing - Christmas	(122)	writing - short story
(93)	proofreading	(108)	spelling/writing	(123)	writing - long adjectives
(94)	spelling/parts of speech	(109)	participle adjectives	(124)	writing - hyphens, semicolons
(95)	proofreading	(110)	writing - short story	(125)	English review
(96)	writing - compare and contrast	(111)	spelling/writing	(126)	writing - fiction
(97)	writing - persuasive essay	(112)	spelling/writing	(127)	writing - fiction
(98)	writing - persuasive essay	(113)	writing - vignette	(128)	writing - fiction
(99)	writing - persuasive essay	(114)	spelling	(129)	writing - fiction
(100)	writing - persuasive essay	(115)	spelling/writing	(130)	writing - fiction
(101)	proofreading	(116)	spelling/writing	(131)	writing - paragraphs
(102)	writing - similes, commas	(117)	spelling/writing	(132)	writing - paragraphs
(103)	writing - quotation marks, clauses	(118)	spelling/writing	(133)	writing - paragraphs
(104)	writing - descriptive	(119)	spelling/parts of speech	(134)	writing - paragraphs
(105)	writing - short story	(120)	spelling/participles	(135)	writing - paragraphs

Completion Chart for Lessons 136-180

(136)	writing - paragraphs	(151)	writing - paragraph	(166)	writing - research project
(137)	writing - paragraphs	(152)	commas	(167)	writing - research project
(138)	writing - paragraphs	(153)	punctuation/ apostrophes	(168)	writing - research project
(139)	writing - paragraphs	(154)	parts of speech	(169)	writing - research project
(140)	writing - paragraphs	(155)	writing - essay	(170)	writing - research project
(141)	common verb mistakes/lie vs. lay	(156)	writing - essay	(171)	writing - research project
(142)	good vs. well/your vs. you're	(157)	writing - essay	(172)	writing - research project
(143)	affect vs. effect/it's vs. its/can vs. may	(158)	writing - essay	(173)	writing - research project
(144)	clauses/better sentences	(159)	writing - essay	(174)	writing - research project
(145)	sentence fragments	(160)	writing - essay	(175)	writing - research project
(146)	sentence fragments	(161)	writing - essay	(176)	writing - research project
(147)	word builder	(162)	editing	(177)	writing - research project
(148)	sentence fragments	(163)	appositives	(178)	writing - research project
(149)	writing - paragraph	(164)	verbs/appositives	(179)	writing - research project
(150)	writing - short story	(165)	commas/combining sentences	(180)	writing - research project

Lesson 1: Following Directions

Can you follow directions? Set a timer for 3 minutes – complete this worksheet within the allotted time! (NOTE: the teaching lesson for this and every worksheet is located in the Lesson Guide. That separate book is necessary to make the course complete.)

1. Read everything thoroughly before you do any step.
2. Put your name in the top right corner of this page.
3. Shout your first name.
4. Circle the word "corner" in step 2.
5. If you have followed the directions so far, yell "Yes!"
6. In the blank space above number 1, write "I can!"
7. Down the left margin, draw five circles.
8. Put a check mark in each circle.
9. Draw a square around each circle.
10. Say the alphabet out loud in order.
11. Count to ten out loud.
12. Count backwards from 10 to 1 out loud.
13. Use the bottom left section to divide 1089 by 11.
14. Circle your answer to number 13.
15. Shout, "I am the master of direction-following!"
16. Use the bottom right section to add 10,820 to 3,999.
17. Draw a triangle around your answer.
18. Draw a rectangle around the triangle.
19. Yell, "I'm almost done and have followed the directions!"
20. Underline all of the even numbers on the whole page.
21. Draw a line through step 14.
22. Now that you've read everything, only do steps 1 and 2!

Lesson 2: Paragraph Predicament • Hangman Language Arts 6

Fix the paragraph below based on these clues: there are 3 spelling mistakes, 2 missing punctuation marks, and 10 capitalization errors.

booker t washington was a great edukator of african americans in the late 1800s and early 1900s. founding thousends of schools throughout the south he knew that education was highly important for the social advancement of his race. He was also a political advisor to both FDR and president taft, and greatly improved the rashul relations in america during his lifetime.

Try to figure out the animal words below in ten guesses or less. Cross out letters you've already guessed to help yourself keep track. Find someone to check your guesses using the answer key.

A B C D E F G H I J K L M N O P Q R S T U V W X Y Z

__ __ __ __ __ __ __

A B C D E F G H I J K L M N O P Q R S T U V W X Y Z

__ __ __ __ __ __ __

Lesson 3: Syllables • Spelling

This is a poem by Carl Sandburg called *Goldwing Moth*. Many of the words only have one syllable. For any multi-syllabic words, draw a line between the syllables.

A goldwing moth is between the scissors and the ink bottle on the desk.

Last night it flew hundreds of circles around a glass bulb and a flame wire.

The wings are a soft gold; it is the gold of illuminated initials in manuscripts of the medieval monks.

Spell these words as they are read to you from the Lesson Guide. Do your best and review any mistakes you make.

_____   _____

_____   _____

_____   _____

_____   _____

_____   _____

Fix the paragraph below based on these clues: there are 3 spelling mistakes, 4 missing punctuation marks, and 5 capitalization errors.

charles lindbergh was fasinated with flying. though trained as a mecanical engineer he is best known for being the first person to fly across the atlantic He did this in 1927, not even twenty five years after the wright bruthers first flight in 1903.

Find your spelling words from lesson 3 in the word search below. Words can be found vertically, horizontally, and diagonally.

```
G A X M E E Y H F B Q H U T S
N N V V F M I U F M T J H K I
C N S E N S A T I O N A L K S
R E I R M T R J Q L W U E L E
U W R A Q O V U C I Q C K A H
T C A E U Z W I R U N N M G T
E V T B A A M E X E T B T O N
O S L C G L D F T J F J J N Y
F E U H E I I S B I K C F Y S
Q F A A S L I W R Q S H T X O
Z S N N C X L S P W S L G Y T
T P O N E E Y O I V W C U X O
Z C A Y O F B X C J G M M O H
Y E X P H E T V U Q G N X U P
I Q D Z A Z K Z T F K Y R B R
```

collect
because
consider
aghast
sensational
agony
trouble
cereal
existence
photo-synthesis

Write a poem in ABAAB form like the example stanza below from *A Road Not Taken* by Robert Frost.

> *Two roads diverged in a yellow wood,*
> *And sorry I could not travel both*
> *And be one traveler, long I stood*
> *And looked down one as far as I could*
> *To where it bent in the undergrowth;*

_____

_____

_____

_____

_____

_____

_____

Think About It   "Poetry is when an emotion has found its thought and the thought has found words."

-Robert Frost

Fix the paragraphs below based on these clues: in total, there are 7 spelling mistakes, 8 missing punctuation marks, and 4 capitalization errors.

Gus Grissom was a pianeer of american space exploration. He was one of the original Mercury Seven and he was the secont american ever to go to space.

Born in 1926 in Mitchell Indiana Grissom was originally a combat pilot in the korean war. He moved on to be an Air Force test pilot, and finally a NASA astronot. He made his first journey into space in 1961 aboard the Liberty Bell 7. In the year 1965 he became the first man in history to make a return trip to space as he journied aboard the Gemini 3. During preparations for his third trip to space Gus Grissom died in a fire during a launch pad test for Apollo 1.

Before his death, Grissom said the following: "If we die we want people to except it. We're in a risky bisness and we hope that if anything happens to us it will not delay the program. The conkuest of space is worth the risk of life.

Write a short story.

_____

_____

_____

_____

_____

_____

_____

_____

_____

_____

Writing Tip: Remember to vary your sentences in type (complex, compound, etc.) and length to make your writing more exciting for your readers.

Lesson 8: Parts of Speech

Circle the part of speech that correctly labels the underlined word in each sentence.

Dancing is my <u>favorite</u> activity.   noun   adverb   adjective

Did that door just shut <u>itself</u>?   verb   pronoun   adverb

The concert <u>was</u> fabulous.   verb   preposition   noun

The morning <u>swim</u> was cold.   noun   verb   adjective

Whose shoes are <u>by</u> the door?   adverb   verb   preposition

Let's go to the library <u>soon</u>.   noun   adverb   pronoun

<u>Chicago</u> gets many visitors.   verb   noun   adjective

She looked <u>very</u> pretty.   adjective   pronoun   adverb

That was a <u>costly</u> mistake.   adverb   verb   adjective

Please help <u>yourself</u> to the fridge.   noun   pronoun   verb

The storm raged <u>during</u> the night.   preposition   verb   noun

Can you <u>chop</u> the vegetables?   verb   noun   adjective

<u>Yesterday</u> was my birthday.   verb   pronoun   adverb

Lesson 9: Grammar Review

Language Arts 6

Of the bolded words, circle the one that matches the part of speech to the side of the sentence

Did you **look through** the **mail yet**? — Preposition

I **hope** to **go** for a **jog** first thing **tomorrow**. — Noun

Her **curly hair** is **fun** to **play** with. — Adjective

I can't **get** all of **this** done **by myself**. — Pronoun

Her **exquisitely designed** cake **won** first **prize**. — Adverb

God's love is **amazing**. — Verb

Head toward the **gas** station and **turn** right. — Preposition

Are **you** up **for** a **leisurely stroll**? — Adjective

I **have** a **hair** appointment **tomorrow morning**. — Adverb

What do **you think** about the **proposal**? — Verb

How can **you** stand to **eat fish**? — Pronoun

His bravery was **astounding**. — Noun

Can you figure out a way to combine the group of sentences into one sentence without losing any of the information?

Louisa May Alcott was homeschooled.
Louisa had a passion for reading.
Louisa wrote over 30 books.
Little Women is her most famous book.

_____

_____

_____

Octaviano Larrazolo was Mexican-born.
Larrazolo was the first Hispanic U.S. Senator.
He represented New Mexico.
He had previously been New Mexico's governor.

_____

_____

_____

The oldest known pair of ice skates date back to 3000 B.C.
They were found at the bottom of a lake in Switzerland.
They were made from the leg bone of a large animal.

_____

_____

_____

Lesson 11: Metaphors

Answer the following questions as a refresher course on metaphors.

We could have people over more often if the *house wasn't such a pigsty.*

This metaphor compares the house to a pigsty because...

    a.   ...we raise pigs.

    b.   ...it stinks like a barn.

    c.   ...it is messy.

I woke up to a *blanket of snow* **on the ground.**

This metaphor compares the snow to a blanket because...

    a.   ...it covered the ground.

    b.   ...it was warm.

    c.   ...it was on the bed.

Emma's legs were Jell-O **as she took her place on the stage.**

This metaphor compares Emma's legs to Jell-O because...

    a.   ...she spilled her snack on them.

    b.   ...they were shaking from her nerves.

    c.   ...she was hungry.

Sam, *the family early bird*, **got the rest of the cereal.**

This metaphor compares Sam to an early bird because...

    a.   ...he liked worms.

    b.   ...he got up before everyone else.

    c.   ...he enjoyed singing in the morning.

Write three metaphors.

_____

_____

_____

_____

_____

_____

_____

_____

Famous Metaphor: "All the world's a stage, and all the men and women merely players."

-William Shakespeare

Lesson 13: Word Scramble

Can you unscramble the letters to correctly spell a word to fit the blank? If you need help, have someone read you the unscrambled words from the answer key and then you can try to spell them correctly.

The ORUMSONE spider made me jump.

_____

We called an IAELICNETRC to fix our fuse.

_____

Being able to keep clean continued to UEELD him.

_____

You have a worried IEPNXEORSS on your face.

_____

Riding a roller coaster fills me with XHOLRATIAENI.

_____

Water is IANTSSEEL for life.

_____

That pianist's talent was RROEATDNAXIYR!

_____

Last night's sunset was absolutely UTQISEIXE.

_____

The project NNGEIREE laid out the plans for the bridge.

_____

I cannot contain my ITXMECNETE about our vacation!

_____

Lesson 14: Sentence Fragments • Proofreading Language Arts 6

Turn the sentence fragments into complete sentences.

The big, scary dog.

_____

Watched the gorgeous sunset.

_____

Her long, curly hair.

_____

Ran down the road.

_____

Across the street.

_____

Select the option that correctly fills in each blank.

They expected _____ to do all of their laundry.

Mom and I   Mom and me

There was _____ much laundry for us to do it all.

to   two   too

_____ did get all of the clean laundry folded, though.

Mom and I   Mom and me

_____ fortunate we were willing to help at all!

Their   There   They're

Lesson 15: Similes

Arts 6

Put an X on the line if the sentence is a simile, and leave it blank if it's not. Then write a simile containing an animal on the lines.

My mom calls me a couch potato. _____

The pillows were fluffy clouds. _____

My brother eats like a pig. _____

She's as light as a feather. _____

He was drowning in a sea of grief. _____

My coach was an ogre when we lost. _____

The car was like a rocket. _____

The book was good food for thought. _____

Her stomach was flipping like a gymnast. _____

Go left at the fork in the road. _____

She was as happy as a clam. _____

They tiptoed like ballerinas. _____

The promise was a steady rock. _____

Her eyes burned like a campfire. _____

The betrayal was a knife in the back. _____

_____

_____

Write about a time when either you treated someone differently because of how they looked or you treated someone the same despite how they looked.

_____

_____

_____

_____

_____

_____

_____

_____

Think About It: "Prejudices, it is well known, are most difficult to eradicate from the heart whose soil has never been loosened or fertilised by education: they grow there, firm as weeds among stones."
                                                              -Charlotte Brontë

Write a simile and a metaphor about yourself.

_____

_____

_____

_____

_____

_____

Writing Tip: While similes and metaphors are big components of poetry, they can also help improve your nonpoetic writing such as stories and essays, making them more interesting for your readers.

Lesson 18: Verbs

Put the correct present tense of the verb in parenthesis into the blank. Make sure to figure out what the subject of the sentence is, and then match the verb to it.

Everyone at the game, including the umpires, _____ that the rain lets up soon. (to hope)

The nights _____ long, but the days _____ short. (to be)

This bread _____ stale to me. (to taste)

My mom, with the help of my dad, _____ mastered the new Lego video game. (to have)

The twelve gallons of milk for the after-play snack _____ it difficult to fit anything else in the fridge. (to make)

The young girl _____ her math facts but has trouble recalling them quickly. (to know)

The finish on our hardwood floors _____ to be replaced due to scratches. (to need)

Each of the children _____ to the park hoping for a free swing. (to come)

The producers of the show _____ the upcoming musical schedule at the end of the show. (to announce)

The audience _____ at the scary parts of the film. (to gasp)

The airplane _____ to the destination at a brisk pace. (to fly)

Lesson 19: Spelling

Fill in the blanks of the story while someone reads it to you from the answer key. Do the best you can to spell them correctly.

_____ about the _____ of

Europe _____ to Mandy. She loved the old

_____ and the beautiful _____.

Travelling on an _____ for hours to get there

even sounded fun! She was antsy with _____

to take a trip there. Unfortunately, due to the large

_____ of such a trip, she would have to be

_____ and save her money for a _____.

Lesson 20: Similes

Match the simile beginning with the ending that makes the most sense. Write the letter of the ending in the blank beside the beginning.

As hungry as _____   a.   nails

As flat as _____   b.   a bee

As solid as _____   c.   a pancake

As quiet as _____   d.   a mouse

As busy as _____   e.   a bat

As cold as _____   f.   dirt

As good as _____   g.   the hills

As blind as _____   h.   a wolf

As tough as _____   i.   a rock

As easy as _____   j.   silk

As poor as _____   k.   ice

As old as _____   l.   gold

As smooth as _____   m.   pie

Lesson 21: Writing - Metaphors

Choose a noun.

_____

Now choose two adjectives to describe that noun.

_____

_____

Use each adjective to write a metaphor about your noun. You should have two metaphors.

_____

_____

_____

_____

Writing Tip: Metaphors may be one of the best ways to make your writing interesting to your readers. Think of ways you can extend a metaphor across multiple sentences. State your metaphor, and then expand on it by describing it further. The more practice you get doing this, the more natural it will become as you write.

Choose a noun.

_____

Now choose two adjectives to describe that noun.

_____

_____

Use each adjective to write a metaphor about your noun. You should have two metaphors.

_____

_____

_____

_____

Extended Metaphor: Lesson 21's tip talked about extending metaphors. Here's an example. *Her hair was a golden waterfall* could extend to *her hair was a golden waterfall, crashing down over her shoulders and bubbling around her waist*. The waterfall description is carried further to make the metaphor more vivid for the reader. Can you extend one of your metaphors above?

Choose the selection that corrects any error that might exist in the underlined portions of the paragraphs. If there is no error, select "no change."

Janine reached into her <u>bag, hoping</u> to find her appointment card. She <u>couldn't remember</u> what time she was supposed to arrive at the dentist. When she finally found <u>it, she</u> realized she had the wrong day!

    a.   bag hoping
    b.   couldn't, remember
    c.   it she
    d.   no change

Luke opened all of his birthday <u>gifts at</u> a frazzled pace. He was hoping to receive the gift he wanted the <u>most a</u> painting from his grandfather. When he opened the last <u>box, his</u> eyes teared up as he saw a portrait of himself staring back at him. His grandfather had an incredible talent.

    a.   gifts, at
    b.   most, a
    c.   box his
    d.   no change

The president of the United <u>States has</u> a tough job. He often has to put his own convictions <u>aside for</u> the good of the country. Any time there's a national <u>problem everyone</u> blames the president. I wouldn't want that job.

    a.   States, has
    b.   aside, for
    c.   problem, everyone
    d.   no change

Lesson 24: Proofreading

Fix the fragments! Choose the selection that corrects any error that might exist in the underlined portions of the paragraphs. If there is no error, select "no change."

The twisty mountain roads made Jordan feel queasy. He loved <u>reading, but</u> he decided it would be smart to put his book <u>down until</u> the roads were straight again. Putting the book <u>down and looking</u> out the window helped him feel better. As a bonus, he got to enjoy the mountain beauty!

    a.   reading but
    b.   down. Until
    c.   down, looking
    d.   no change

The essay assignment loomed in front of Andrew. He freely <u>admitted. Writing</u> didn't come easily to him, so he always put writing assignments off until the last minute. His mom gently pointed out that if he'd do them a little bit at a <u>time, they'd</u> be much easier to complete. He knew she was <u>right, and</u> he decided to buckle down and get to work.

    a.   admitted writing
    b.   time. They'd
    c.   right. And
    d.   no change

The Statue of Liberty has been a welcome sight for many immigrants across the years. As they arrived at nearby Ellis <u>Island, they</u> would see the statue and know they were entering a land of freedom and <u>democracy. Standing</u> over 151 feet <u>tall. It</u> is a quintessential emblem of liberty, known throughout the world.

    a.   Island. They
    b.   democracy, standing
    c.   tall, it
    d.   no change

Fix the paragraph below based on these clues: there are 10 spelling mistakes and 5 punctuation errors.

When you put a piece of food into your mouth dijestion begins. As you choo your food saliva helps break it down further. Once you swallow food travells through your esophagus and enters your stomuck where dijestive juices break it down even more.   From the stomuck food travells further into the small intestin where nutrients are absorbed. What is left enters the large intestin where water is absorbed and waste is stored?

Use the blank to write the correct plural form of the word in parentheses.

Can you hand me all of the (knife) _____?

Those (person) _____ aren't being very quiet in the library.

There must have been eight (deer) _____ on that hill!

My aunt's house has a problem with (mouse) _____.

The (mosquito) _____ are out in full force this evening.

The school had a wide variety for our (lunch) _____.

Fix the paragraph below based on these clues: there are 5 spelling mistakes, 7 punctuation errors, and 2 capitalization errors.

Synonyms are words with symilar meanings! antonims on the other hand are words with opposite meanings. For instance cold and hot are antonims but Cold and chilly are synonyms. A good way to remember them is to think that synonym sounds a little like symilar and if you're anti-something, you're opposed to it. Can you think of examples of synonyms and antonims.

Fill in the blanks with the plural of the given word. The right column is harder. Learn from any mistakes you make.

theory   _____   alga   _____

shelf   _____   stimulus _____

piano   _____   index   _____

cliff   _____   thesis _____

hitch   _____   medium _____

hero   _____   series _____

Write about an imaginary country.

_____

_____

_____

_____

_____

_____

_____

_____

_____

Fun Fact: In Mongolia, sheep outnumber humans 35 to 1. Did you write any fun facts about your country?

Lesson 28: Spelling

Spell these words as they are read to you from the Lesson Guide. Do your best and review any mistakes you make.

_____   _____

_____   _____

_____   _____

_____   _____

_____   _____

_____   _____

_____   _____

_____   _____

Write an example of dialogue that uses a speech tag.

_____

_____

_____

Write an example of dialogue that uses a descriptive tag.

_____

_____

_____

Write an example of dialogue that uses an action tag.

_____

_____

_____

Lesson 30: Writing - Dialogue Language Arts 6

Write a dialogue between yourself and a character from a book you are reading.

_____

_____

_____

_____

_____

_____

_____

_____

_____

Writing Tip: Varying your dialogue tags between speech, descriptive, and action, as well as mixing up where you put the tags in your sentences will make your dialogues more engaging for your readers.

Write a sentence that applies the comma rule about two independent clauses joined by a connector such as *and*, *or*, or *but*.

_____

_____

_____

Write a sentence that applies the comma rule about expressions that interrupt the sentence flow.

_____

_____

_____

Write a sentence that applies the comma rule about cities and their states.

_____

_____

_____

What has been the most entertaining part so far of a book you are reading? Thoroughly explain why it's the most entertaining in your opinion.

_____

_____

_____

_____

_____

_____

_____

_____

_____

Writing Tip: It always makes your writing stronger and more engaging when you back up your opinions and facts with supporting details.

For each of the following, choose the sentence that has the correct comma usage.

a. You are, I'm certain, going to be great!
b. You are I'm certain going to be great!
c. You are I'm certain, going to be great!

a. Penelope, and Jason, each brought milk to the breakfast.
b. Penelope and Jason, each brought milk to the breakfast.
c. Penelope and Jason each brought milk to the breakfast.

a. I'm speaking Sarah, so I'd like you to be quiet.
b. I'm speaking, Sarah, so I'd like you to be quiet.
c. I'm speaking Sarah so I'd like you to be quiet.

a. Please get your shoes, jacket, and scarf off the living room floor.
b. Please get your shoes, jacket, and scarf, off the living room floor.
c. Please get, your shoes, jacket, and scarf off the living room floor.

a. My mom Gail is the one you're looking for.
b. My mom Gail, is the one you're looking for.
c. My mom, Gail, is the one you're looking for.

a. Though the storm lasted all night, I slept like a baby.
b. Though the storm lasted all night I slept like a baby.
c. Though, the storm lasted all night, I slept like a baby.

Lesson 34: Writing

Using a book you are reading, find and copy a simple sentence.

_____

_____

_____

Using a book you are reading, find and copy a compound sentence.

_____

_____

_____

Using a book you are reading, find and copy a complex sentence.

_____

_____

_____

Fun Fact: The word *set* has 464 different definitions in the dictionary. Talk about complex!

Write about a day you spend in a setting from the book you are currently reading.

_____

_____

_____

_____

_____

_____

_____

_____

_____

Lesson 36: Simple, Compound, or Complex   Language Arts 6

For each of the following sentences, select which type of sentence is used.

Your bedroom smells like dirty laundry.

      simple   compound   complex

Although I wash your clothes, you should put them in the hamper yourself.

      simple   compound   complex

I see dirty socks under your bed, and I see a towel wadded up in the corner.

      simple   compound   complex

Could you please get it all to the laundry room?

      simple   compound   complex

I'm about to start a load anyway, and I'd like for your stuff to be included.

      simple   compound   complex

You'll notice an immediate difference in your room.

      simple   compound   complex

Besides smelling fresher, your room will be cleaner, too.

      simple   compound   complex

Choose a famous event and rewrite it in your own way. Give it a twist that didn't actually happen in history.

_____

_____

_____

_____

_____

_____

_____

_____

_____

_____

Fill in the blanks of the story as someone reads it to you from the answer key.

I asked my mom for some _____ about an

upcoming babysitting job. I was nervous because it was

my first one with a preschooler. As she put away the

_____, she chose to _____ me

about keeping him occupied. "Try _____,"

she suggested, "or even make music with your old

_____." I could feel my _____

begin to _____ at her great suggestions.

Can you figure out a way to combine the group of sentences into one sentence without losing any of the information?

Albert Einstein often daydreamed in class during school.

He daydreamed because so many ideas filled his mind.

He went on to graduate with a degree in physics.

He is probably the most famous physicist of the 20th century.

_____

_____

_____

_____

Einstein is most famous for his theory of relativity.

This theory asserts that E equals mc squared.

This stands for energy equals mass times the speed of light squared.

_____

_____

_____

Lesson 40: Commas

Choose the selection that corrects any error that might exist in the underlined portions of the sentences. If there is no error, select "no change."

The drink <u>selections for</u> the evening <u>are, Dr</u> Pepper, Diet Coke, Sprite, <u>water, or</u> iced tea.

      a.   selections, for
      b.   are Dr
      c.   water; or
      d.   no change

Thank <u>you, Sandra,</u> for taking the <u>time, however</u> <u>brief, to</u> explain the diagram to us.

      a.   you Sandra
      b.   time however
      c.   brief to
      d.   no change

The wind blew <u>swiftly, across</u> the <u>yard, picking</u> up leaves and swirling them around until they <u>landed, ready</u> to be picked up again.

      a.   swiftly across
      b.   yard picking
      c.   landed ready
      d.   no change

The leash <u>jingled as</u> I picked it <u>up, signaling</u> to my dog that it was time to take our evening <u>walk his</u> favorite activity.

      a.   jingled, as
      b.   up signaling
      c.   walk, his
      d.   no change

Lesson 41: Spelling

Fill in the missing letter for the words below. Some are easy, some are hard!

s__eve

lett__ce

absen__e

crit__cize

hum__rous

presen__e

para__hute

We__nesday

stren__th

suppose__ly

li__ense

gover__ment

desp__rate

loo__e

spe__ial

def__nite

m__sterious

camo__flage

tom__rrow

comp__tition

w__ether

sold__er

pr__fer

interf__re

independ__nce

def__nitely

Feb__uary

sle__ve

adverti__e

__fficial

med__cine

spe__ch

su__prise

ans__er

resta__rant

recogni__e

ju__gment

exist__nce

basic__lly

Lesson 42: Combining Sentences

Can you figure out a way to combine the group of sentences into one sentence without losing any of the information?

Johan Guttenberg invented the printing press.
He invented it in the 1400s.
It used movable metal letters making printing much quicker.

_____

_____

_____

Before the invention of the printing press, printing was done by hand.
Printing by hand was painstaking.
Materials used for printing included clay, papyrus, wax, and parchment.

_____

_____

_____

After the printing press, knowledge could spread quickly.
As quickly as books could be printed, knowledge could spread.
This caused an eruption of innovation we know as the Renaissance.

_____

_____

_____

Lesson 43: Writing

Copy the best sentence from a chapter you have recently read.

_____

_____

_____

_____

What makes it the best sentence from the chapter?

_____

_____

_____

Now label the parts of speech in your sentence using colors or symbols. Make a key below to show what each color or symbol is labeling.

_____

_____

_____

What type of sentence is it?   simple   compound   complex

Lesson 44: Independent Clauses

How many independent clauses are in the following sentences? Answer the questions about each sentence.

My mom told me to take the dog outside and do my chores before I watched a movie.
- ◯ There are no independent clauses.
- ◯ This sentence has one independent clause.
- ◯ This sentence has two independent clauses.

My mom was worried **that I would forget to do my work**.
- ◯ The bold part of the sentence is the independent clause.
- ◯ The non-bold part of the sentence is the independent clause.
- ◯ This sentence has no independent clause.

I tend to rush my work sometimes; I really love watching movies.
- ◯ There are no independent clauses.
- ◯ This sentence has one independent clause.
- ◯ This sentence has two independent clauses.

My favorite movie, **one based on a book**, has a lot of great actors.
- ◯ The bold part of the sentence is an independent clause.
- ◯ The bold part of the sentence is not an independent clause.
- ◯ This sentence has two independent clauses.

That I can't watch a movie without doing my work.
- ◯ There are no independent clauses.
- ◯ This sentence has one independent clause.
- ◯ This sentence has two independent clauses.

Use this page to jot down quotes and examples from the book you'd like to use for your poster. Be sure to include the page numbers where you find them!

Quote/Example   Page #

_____

_____

_____

_____

_____

_____

_____

_____

_____

_____

Use this page to take notes as you research the author of your book.

Name: _____

Born: _____   Died: _____

Birthplace: _____

Childhood: _____

_____

_____

_____

Education: _____

_____

_____

Other books written: _____

_____

_____

Lesson 47: Book Poster

Write a short summary of your book.

_____

_____

_____

_____

_____

_____

_____

Lesson 51: Dialogue • Writing

Properly punctuate the dialogue at the top of the page. Then use the lines at the bottom of the page to copy the interesting quote by your historical person.

Come here he said

She got up and crossed the room What is it

A geode.

She asked again And that is what exactly

He brought out a hammer Watch and see.

Quote:_____

_____

_____

_____

Author: _____

Date written: _____

Source: _____

_____

(This page left intentionally blank)

Cut out the following pieces and arrange them into different dialogues. Don't forget to use the rules you've learned.

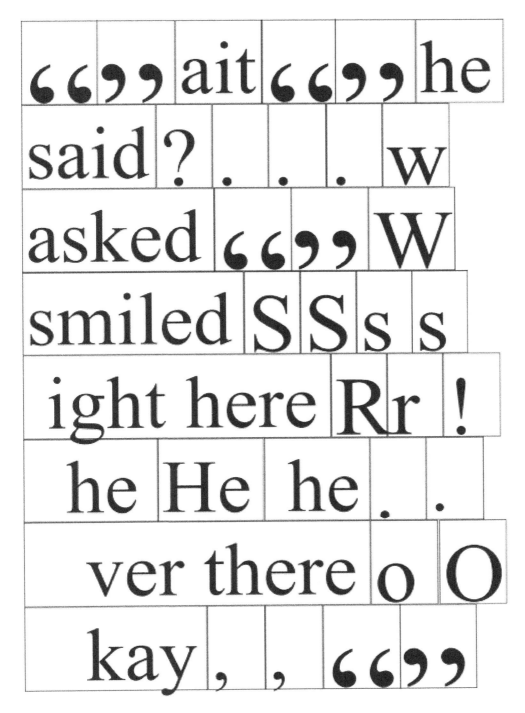

(continued after blank page)

(This page left intentionally blank)

Use this page to write ten facts about your historical person.

1. _____

_____

2. _____

_____

3. _____

_____

4. _____

_____

5. _____

_____

6. _____

_____

7. _____

_____

8. _____

_____

9. _____

_____

10. _____

_____

(This page left intentionally blank)

Lesson 53: Capitalization

Cut out as one piece. Fold in each side and crease. Cut along the dotted lines. Inside each flap write at least one example of each. (Name titles would be Aunt Jenny or President Obama, whereas titles would be aunt and president.)

common nouns things	places	prepositions and insignificant words in titles	titles	first word in the second part of an interrupted quote

Proper Nouns Names of Things	Names of Places	Significant Words in Titles (e.g. book titles)	Name Titles With Names or As Names	The First Word of a Quotation

(This page left intentionally blank)

Lesson 55: Comma Rules • Writing

Write an example of each rule on the line that follows it.

Rule #1 Use a comma to separate things in a series or list.

_____

Rule #2 Use a comma before a conjunction (and, or, but, so) when they separate independent clauses.

_____

Rule #3 Use a comma to separate introductory words in a sentence.

_____

Rule #4 Use a comma to set apart appositives and other unnecessary information.

_____

Rule #5 Use a comma to separate adjectives if you could say "and" in between them.

_____

Rule #6 Use a comma to separate quotes from speech tags.

_____

Rule #7 Use a comma to set apart phrases that express contrast.

_____

Rule #8 Use a comma to avoid confusion.

_____

Rule # 9 Use a comma between city and state, date and year.

_____

Rule #10 Never use only one comma between a subject and its verb.

_____

(continued on next page)

Write a dialogue between the person you chose for your biography essay and another historical character.

Refresh yourself on comma rules by correcting each sentence according to the rule that precedes it.

Rule #1 Use a comma to separate things in a series or list.

I used to ride bikes skip rope run races and roll in the grass.

Rule #2 Use a comma before a conjunction (and, or, but, so) when they separate independent clauses.

Now I cook and clean and my kids do all those things.

Rule #3 Use a comma to separate introductory words in a sentence.

When I was young I thought being old would be fun.

Rule #4 Use a comma to set apart appositives and other unnecessary information.

Now that I'm old as if thirty-seven is old I think I was right.

Rule #5 Use a comma to separate adjectives if you could say "and" in between them.

I have a bunch of fun energetic creative kids.

Rule #6 Use a comma to separate quotes from speech tags.

"It's tomorrow" my son says in the mornings.

Rule #7 Use a comma to set apart phrases that express contrast.

We try and explain that it's today not tomorrow.

Rule #8 Use a comma to avoid confusion.

He'll jump up and say, "Let's eat Mom!"

Rule # 9 Use a comma between city and state, date and year.

We haven't lived near Philadelphia Pennsylvania since May 31 2002.

Rule #10 Never use only one comma between a subject and its verb.

Riding a bike is something you never forget how to do.

(continued on next page)

Write a comedy dialogue.

_____

_____

_____

_____

_____

_____

_____

_____

_____

_____

Lesson 59: Sentence Types

Select which sentence type describes the sentence given.

What a fantastic day!
○ declarative   ○ interrogative   ○ exclamatory   ○ imperative

Where do you keep the bandages?
○ declarative   ○ interrogative   ○ exclamatory   ○ imperative

My brother is a 6'5" basketball sensation.
○ declarative   ○ interrogative   ○ exclamatory   ○ imperative

Please stop screaming.
○ declarative   ○ interrogative   ○ exclamatory   ○ imperative

What is all over your shirt?
○ declarative   ○ interrogative   ○ exclamatory   ○ imperative

When I was little, I really enjoyed riding my bike.
○ declarative   ○ interrogative   ○ exclamatory   ○ imperative

I can't believe she said that!
○ declarative   ○ interrogative   ○ exclamatory   ○ imperative

What would you like for lunch?
○ declarative   ○ interrogative   ○ exclamatory   ○ imperative

Keep your hands to yourself.
○ declarative   ○ interrogative   ○ exclamatory   ○ imperative

It's really hot in here today.
○ declarative   ○ interrogative   ○ exclamatory   ○ imperative

Look out!
○ declarative   ○ interrogative   ○ exclamatory   ○ imperative

Write an advertisement for the (pretend) band the main character of your book is in. You can use the box to make a mini poster advertising the band if you'd like.

_____

_____

_____

_____

_____

_____

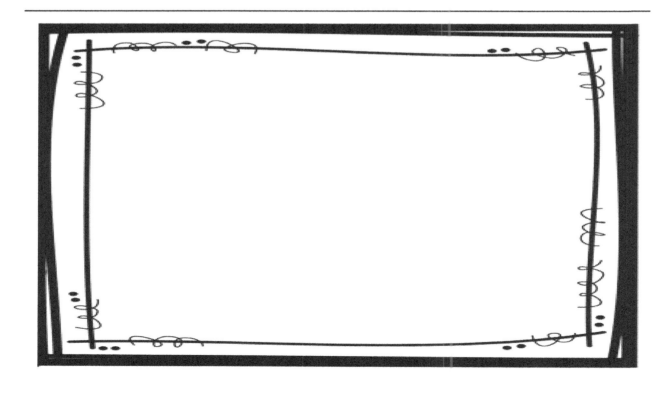

Lesson 64: Editing Checklist

Read through your essay and fix any mistakes. Here is an editing checklist. Aim for a check mark in each box.

Introduction
- ☐ My introduction begins with an attention grabber.
- ☐ My introduction has at least three sentences.
- ☐ My introduction ends with the main idea of my essay.

Body
- ☐ The body of my essay has at least three paragraphs.
- ☐ Each paragraph of the body starts with a topic sentence.
- ☐ Each paragraph of the body has at least three supporting sentences.
- ☐ Each paragraph of the body has a conclusion sentence.

Conclusion
- ☐ My conclusion has at least three sentences.
- ☐ My conclusion restates my main idea.
- ☐ My conclusion answers the question, "So what?"

Unity
- ☐ My essay flows well and makes sense.
- ☐ My essay uses transition words.
- ☐ My essay is interesting.

Subject Matter
- ☐ My essay has different sentences – short, long, compound, complex.
- ☐ My essay uses descriptive words.
- ☐ All parts of my essay support my main idea.

Grammar/Mechanics
- ☐ All words are spelled correctly.
- ☐ There are no grammatical mistakes.
- ☐ There are no punctuation errors.
- ☐ There are no fragments.
- ☐ There are no run-on sentences.

Write a letter to your mother from the time period you are studying in history.

_____

_____

_____

_____

_____

_____

_____

_____

_____

_____

Writing Tip: Mark Twain once said, "The secret of getting ahead is getting started." Get in the habit of writing a little bit each day and you'll be ahead in your writing.

Fix the paragraphs below based on the clues given.

This paragraph has 3 spelling mistakes, 4 missing punctuation marks, and 2 capitalization errors.

Paper-making has come a long weigh over the centuries. First trees are harvested and sent to the mill. Next logs are sent threw a machine that strips them of there bark. eventually the pulp is soaked and then pressed together and dried automated machines can make huge rolls of thin paper that can be cut into whatever size is needed.

This paragraph has 4 spelling mistakes and 3 missing punctuation marks.

Their are three main types of rock. Sedimentary rocks are maid up of layers of sediment that have compacted together over time. Igneous rocks are formed when magma cools and hardens. Sometimes they form inside the earths surface. Other times they form on the surface after a volcanic eruption expels them. Metamorphic rocks are rocks that used to be one of the other too types and changed do to things like weather heat and pressure.

Lesson 67: Parts of Speech

Use something to cover the paragraph at the bottom of the page while you fill out the blanks at the top according to the part of speech indicated. Then uncover the story and use the words at the top to fill in the blanks. Was your story silly?

1. adjective: _____

2. noun: _____

3. ing verb: _____

4. place: _____

5. collective noun: _____

6. exclamation: _____

7. past tense verb: _____

8. adjective: _____

Don't peek until you've filled out the top section!

Yesterday was my birthday. When I woke up, my mom had cooked ____(1)____ ____(2)____ for breakfast. I couldn't believe it! Then she said we would be ____(3)____ to the ____(4)____ as my gift from her and my dad. When we got home, a huge ____(5)____ had gathered. "____(6)____!" they all ____(7)____. It was a ____(8)____ birthday.

Read through your book report and fix any mistakes. Here is an editing checklist. Aim for a check mark in each box.

Introduction
- ☐ My introduction begins with an attention grabber.
- ☐ My introduction has at least three sentences.
- ☐ My introduction ends with the main idea of my essay.

Body
- ☐ The body of my essay has at least three paragraphs.
- ☐ Each paragraph of the body starts with a topic sentence.
- ☐ Each paragraph of the body has at least three supporting sentences.
- ☐ Each paragraph of the body has a conclusion sentence.

Conclusion
- ☐ My conclusion has at least three sentences.
- ☐ My conclusion restates my main idea.
- ☐ My conclusion answers the question, "So what?"

Unity
- ☐ My paper flows well and makes sense.
- ☐ My paper uses transition words.
- ☐ My paper is interesting.

Subject Matter
- ☐ My paper has different sentences – short, long, compound, complex.
- ☐ My paper uses descriptive words.
- ☐ All parts of my paper support my main idea.

Grammar/Mechanics
- ☐ All words are spelled correctly.
- ☐ There are no grammatical mistakes.
- ☐ There are no punctuation errors.
- ☐ There are no fragments.
- ☐ There are no run-on sentences.

Underline the adjectives in the sentences below. If you need help, try to find the nouns first, and then underline the words that are describing them. There are multiple adjectives in each sentence.

The small, yippy dog barked well into the summer night.

The young mom brought her newborn baby to the doctor.

My helpful brother will happily carry your heavy bags.

Whose striped bag is sitting on the filthy floor?

Stephanie lost her purple ring after three months.

The baby zebra galloped across the dusty terrain.

That dog has beautiful fur.

The colorful graphics made the computer game extra fun.

The popcorn ceiling left white flakes in my hair as I painted it.

My cozy bed is loudly calling my name at the end of this day.

We had a delicious dinner of juicy steak and mashed potatoes.

The quick brown fox jumped over the lazy dog.

The colorful leaves fell to the cold ground in the gentle breeze.

Lesson 73: Formal Letter

Write a letter to the president. Use a formal letter writing format like the example.

_____

_____

_____

_____

_____

_____

_____

_____

_____

_____

_____

123 Any Street
Anytown, USA 01234

May 15, 2060

President USA
1600 Pennsylvania Avenue
Washington, D.C. 20500

Dear Mr. President:

I just wanted to thank you for keeping the right to homeschool such an important part of your presidency. Every person should have the right to be educated in the way that best fits them. I'm sure you're aware of the many who've held your office before you who were homeschooled. Even as late as FDR, homeschooling has been an important part of our nation's history and heritage. Keep up the good work!

Sincerely,
Sue Smith
Student

Lesson 74: Adjective Quiz

Answer the following questions about adjectives. Learn from any mistakes!

Which word in this sentence is an adjective?
The doctor gave a prescription to the sickly girl.

      a. doctor   b. gave   c. prescription   d. sickly

Which bolded word is not an adjective?
    a. I'm **perfectly** capable of cooking dinner.
    b. I can make several **delicious** meals.
    c. The problem is, I don't find cooking to be a **fun** activity.
    d. So I tend to have lots of **simple** sandwiches and bowls of cereal.

Which of the choices is the correct form of the superlative for the sentence?
That was the _____ nap I've ever had.
    a. peaceful
    b. peacefulest
    c. most peaceful
    d. most peacefulest

Which choice correctly completes the sentence?
Your creative ability is _____ than mine.
    a. best
    b. more better
    c. gooder
    d. better

Which words correctly complete the sentence?
_____ trees _____ really blooming this spring.
    a. That… is
    b. Those… are
    c. The… is
    d. This… are

What is the correct way to write the proper adjective in the sentence?
The north american continent has a wide array of weather.
    a. North american
    b. North American
    c. north American
    d. north american

Write a letter from a child from the time period you are studying in history.

_____

_____

_____

_____

_____

_____

_____

_____

_____

September, 1860

Dear Pa,

I know it will be a long time before you get this letter, but I wanted to write and tell you how much I miss you. Ma, Patricia, and I are doing well, but we miss you like crazy. We know you had to go back and help the others venture west, but we can't wait for you to be with us again. We pray daily for your safety.

You should have seen the size of the rabbit I snagged for dinner last night! It was the biggest one I've ever seen. We were able to share some meat with a few others, and Ma says the skins will make a nice, warm blanket for Patricia to use come winter. I'm doing my best to take care of them. I know you would be proud.

I'd better get this letter sealed and ready for transport. Daniel is traveling to meet the Pony Express rider in the morning, and I want to make sure this letter gets to you before you leave to come back to us.

Much love,

Jimmy

Lesson 76: Advertising

For each example given, write on the line which type of advertising is being demonstrated.

A used car dealership lists a minivan online for $2,999. When you get to the lot, you notice that the cheapest vehicle they have available is $5,999.

_____

A magazine ad for chips speaks of how their bags contain 20% more than "the other guy." (Of course, the ad doesn't mention that their bag also costs 20% more.)

_____

A television commercial for a smartphone invites you to "be yourself" and switch to their "unique" phone.

_____

A radio advertisement for an internet provider implores you to "join the millions of people who have made the switch."

_____

An internet banner ad displays a picture of a popular teen actor flashing his pearly whites while holding a particular brand's tube of whitening toothpaste.

_____

A full page newspaper ad shows a farmer in overalls standing in front of a truck. An American flag is behind him and the ad touts that the truck is "proudly American made for everyday Americans like you."

_____

Write, draw, or create an ad using the questions in the Lesson Guide to help you make it effective. If you'd like to draw, use the blank space at the bottom.

_____

_____

_____

_____

_____

Use the ad at the bottom of the page to answer these questions.

What is the message of the advertisement? _____

_____

_____

What persuasive techniques is the advertisement using? _____

_____

_____

Who is the target audience of the advertisement?_____

_____

Is the ad effective? Why or why not?

_____

_____

_____

_____

Lesson 79: Advertising

Use this chart to compare and contrast your two commercials.

	First Commercial	Second Commercial
Product		
Message		
Target Audience		
Persuasive Technique(s) Used (give examples from the commercials)		
Intended Effect		

Write a commercial using what you've learned about advertising.

_____

_____

_____

_____

_____

_____

_____

_____

_____

_____

Think it Through: What persuasive technique did you use in your commercial? Can you identify any? Did you use more than one? How will this help your product sell?

Lesson 81: Funny Story

Draw your main character for a funny story you are going to write. Use the lines to write a bit about him or her. Make sure to give your character a name and age.

_____

_____

_____

_____

_____

Lesson 82: Parts of Speech

Of the bolded words, underline the one that matches the part of speech to the side of the sentence.

Would **you** like **to** go **to** the **store** with me?   Preposition

Tomorrow is my brother's **golden birthday**.   Noun

The **novel** was so **thick it seemed** unending.   Adjective

The **wind made** the door **seem** to shut **itself**.   Pronoun

The **long line** took us **long into** the night.   Adverb

My sister **is** the world's **best** ballet **dancer**.   Verb

Circle the part of speech that correctly labels the underlined word in each sentence.

My <u>green</u> blanket is so cozy.   noun   adverb   adjective

Please put <u>it</u> down on the table.   verb   pronoun   adverb

I finally <u>watched</u> the program.   verb   preposition   noun

Did you take a sip of my <u>drink</u>?   noun   verb   adjective

The dog jumped <u>out</u> the window!   adverb   verb   preposition

The church steeple rises <u>high</u>.   noun   adverb   pronoun

Lesson 83: Funny Story

Use these three boxes to plot out your funny story. What's going to happen in the beginning, middle, and end?

Circle the part of speech that correctly labels the underlined word in each sentence.

Her manners <u>greatly</u> pleased him. noun adverb adjective

Please <u>place</u> it gently on the counter. verb noun adverb

The bridge collapsed <u>into</u> the river. verb preposition noun

The <u>golden</u> sun crested the horizon. noun verb adjective

Her <u>walk</u> was more of a waddle. verb noun preposition

The bird bumped <u>its</u> beak on the door. noun verb pronoun

Of the bolded words, underline the one that matches the part of speech to the side of the sentence.

We **went** for a **walk after dinner**. Preposition

The **softball** didn't feel **soft** when it **hit my** nose. Noun

It **took** a **long** time to **drive** to **Milwaukee**. Adjective

I'm not **sure Mr.** Lawson **liked his** gift. Pronoun

My **schedule** is **clear**, so let's **get** together **soon**. Adverb

The dog **delighted** the **crowd** with **his tricks**. Verb

Write a description of the main character of a book or story you are reading. Use as much detail as you can.

_____

_____

_____

_____

_____

_____

_____

_____

_____

Choose the correct homophone to fit the blanks in the sentences.

_____ completely ready to go?

      whose   who's

The girls needed to clean _____ room before playing.

      there   they're   their

There's _____ much snow in the forecast for November!

      too   two   to

Would you like the last _____ of pie?

      peace   piece

I saw a _____ scamper into the woods.

      doe   dough

I am _____ explaining this to you.

      threw   through

I got my hair _____ a darker color last week.

      died   dyed

My dad spent the weekend fixing our van's _____.

      brakes   breaks

My little brother is _____ years old today.

      eight   ate

Will you help me _____ these books to the garage?

      hall   haul

Lesson 88: Subject vs. Object Pronouns

Choose the correct pronoun to fill in the blank. If you need help, try to determine if the needed pronoun should be a subject or an object pronoun.

The boys tried to beat _____ at chess.

    Rachel and I   Rachel and me

Mom is visiting family, so feel free to write _____ and Aunt Carrie a letter.

    she   her

I saw the one who took your pencil. It was _____, that boy in the blue.

    he   him

_____ wore matching sweaters to the fair.

   Her and I   She and I   Her and me

It could have been _____ who raked our yard in kindness.

    he   him

_____ switch desks almost every day.

   She and Lucy   Lucy and her

Dad sat between _____ and Jessie so they wouldn't fight.

    she   her

Matthew realized that neither _____ nor James was ready for the big trip.

    he   him

Becky asked Iris and Denise to come sit by _____.

   she and Lillian   Lillian and her

Choose the correct pronoun to fill in the blank.

My two-year-old insists on getting dressed _____.

       himself   hisself   his self

_____ look exactly alike.

    Her and her father   She and her father   Her father and herself

Either _____ or Michelle will pick you up today.

       he   him   himself

_____ incessant screaming is giving me a headache.

     There   Theirs   Their

It was _____ who ate all of the chips yesterday.

      she   her   herself

Can you give the letter to _____ or Jake?

      they   them   themselves

I wish I was better at basketball than _____.

      he   him   himself

Since Justin is the messiest one here, I assume the trash on the floor is _____.

     his   his'   theirs

We found _____ hiding under the desk.

     she   her   herself

Would you ask _____ if he wants something to drink?

     he   him   himself

Choose the correct pronoun to fill in the blank.

It was _____ who did the dishes for you.

       me   myself   I

My mom asked my sister and _____ to clean our room.

       me   myself   I

Liz and _____ spent the entire day on the computer.

       me   myself   I

My mom was not happy with _____ rearranging the living room furniture without asking.

       me   myself   my

Between you and _____, that movie could have been a lot better.

       me   myself   I

Amy was surprised I spent all night on the phone with _____.

       She and Jenna   Jenna and her

The ringing cellphone in my pocket gave away _____ hiding spot for hide and seek.

       Jennifer's and my   Me and Jennifer's   Myself and Jennifer's

Are you upset with _____ choosing of the read aloud?

       me   myself   my

When it comes to cooking, you know more than _____.

       me   mines   I

See if you can find all of the mistakes in this paragraph without any clues.

Your halfway through this course. What kinds of things have you learned this year. You've learned lots of things about commas. For instance they should go after introductory words in a sentence. You've learned about homophones and are learning witch ones are witch. You've done lots of proofreading, spotting errers in spelling and grammar throughout many sentences and paragrafs. You're writing has improved as you've written essays book reports short stories and more. You know that metaphors use like or as and similes say something is something else. You know better than me where a subject pronoun goes and where an object pronoun goes. And the best part of it all is, you are learning from your mistakes. Its okay to get things wrong just keep learning. I wonder what the second half of the coarse will hold.

Insert the semicolons in the correct spots in the sentences below.

It's hot today therefore, you won't need your jacket.

You should do the dishes then you can play video games.

My sister is older than me my brother is younger than me.

Wash your hands first then you can help me cook.

Let's go to Frosty's they have good pizza.

Something is flashing in the sky perhaps it's an airplane.

This is a good book someone worked hard on it.

I enjoy writing math, on the other hand, is hard for me.

You wash the car I'll vacuum it out.

We don't have cable we prefer to watch movies on DVD.

Your room is a mess you should clean it immediately.

Please leave your shoes outside I just had the carpets cleaned.

My father is taller my mother is shorter.

Australia is an island Austria is landlocked.

My grandfather is lonely we're visiting him tomorrow.

I'll sweep the kitchen you switch the laundry.

Let's charge our phones there's a storm coming.

Correct the mistakes in each sentence using the clues given.

These sentences each have 2 spelling mistakes and 1 punctuation mistake.

Have you scene my small striped, collered shirt?

Mr Henderson drunk too full bottles of water.

I can't beleeve its almost Christmas Eave.

Can you please showe me wear the bathroom is.

The teenagers came too the soup kitchen to voluntear

These sentences have 4 total mistakes.

Hurricane harvey devestated houston in 2017

The heard of cows, were eating grass in the pasteur.

Weather you like it or knot we will be flying in a plain.

You need the doe while I sprinkle in more flower

"Wont you calm down I asked my screaming brother?

Can you find the mistakes in these sentences without any clues?

The dog eight it's food so fast it almost choaked.

I cent an email, did you receive it.

It panes me to sea you so hurt and upset

The boy girl and dog went jogging to the park.

The quiz was a suprise to Brandy and I.

Which choice correctly spells a word?

be_____e   sp_____e   p_____e

liev   leev   leav   erkl   arkl   ark   ree   lupe   ranc

de_____e   pe_____e   c_____e

rel   cid   lve   rceiv   lvic   nter   laf   ren   raz

k_____e   m_____e   r_____e

nowl   nif   ing   auv   aybe   arch   elive   ealiz   ainb

Use something to cover the paragraph at the bottom of the page while you fill out the blanks below according to the part of speech indicated. Then uncover the story and use your words to fill in the blanks. Was your story silly?

1. adjective: _____

2. plural noun: _____

3. ing verb: _____

4. ly adverb: _____

5. adjective: _____

Don't peek until you've filled out the top section!

We took a field trip to the zoo. The _____(1)_____

_____(2)_____ were my favorite. They kept

_____(3)_____ from tree to tree as ____(4)____

as they could. It was such a _____(5)_____ day.

Fix the paragraph below based on these clues: there are 4 spelling mistakes, 10 missing punctuation marks, and 14 capitalization errors.

On december 16 1773 arguably the most famous tee party in history took place. The british had imposed a new tax on all tea imports and the american colonists were angry and frustrated at the amount of taxes being levied upon them. A few radical colonists disgised themselves as mohawk indians took 342 crates of tea from three different british ships and through them into boston harbor. In an attempt to get even the british shut off trade from boston until the cost of the tea should be repaid. However insted of getting what they wanted this move only served to strengthen the colonists resolve to form a separate independent nation. The so-called boston tea party was a big stepping stone toward the revolutionary war.

Use this page to write your compare and contrast paragraph.

_____

_____

_____

_____

_____

_____

_____

_____

Mix it Up   It's easy to use opinions when you're comparing and contrasting your feelings about an issue with someone else's. Can you intersperse facts into your paragraph as well? Using facts to back up your opinions will make your argument more persuasive.

The following chart is one way to brainstorm. You can remember the steps using the acronym FIRES. Fill in the chart below as it pertains to your persuasive essay.

	Topic 1	Topic 2	Topic 3
Facts			
Incidents			
Reasons			
Examples			
Statistics			

Lesson 100: Persuasive Writing Critique

How did you do on your persuasive essay? Fill out this critique.

Skill	Points Possible	Points Received
Audience analysis (you know your audience and address them persuasively)	10	
Evidence (you gave evidence to prove your point)	20	
Consistent appeal used (you chose one appeal and used it throughout: testimonial, bandwagon, etc.)	20	
Spelling (your spelling was correct)	10	
Grammar (you used proper grammar)	10	
Use of interesting words (you used adjectives and adverbs, different length sentences, etc.)	10	
Topic covered (you covered your topic completely and didn't veer from your topic)	15	
Sequence and flow (your paper flowed, used transition words between paragraphs, etc.)	15	
Total	100	
Notes		

Correct the following paragraph by underlining words that need to be capitalized, correctly spelling misspelled words, and filling in any missing punctuation.

We went on a field trip to Mrs Rileys farm last year. Mrs Rileys chicken supplies are family with fresh eggs so my mom thought it would be fun to see the rest of the farm. It had reigned a lot the week before we went to the farm and their was to much mud for my taste as a result. However Mrs. Riley said the pigs really liked all of the mud. Eye don't no why they like it so much. One pig ran past my leg and I shouted ew as it sprayed me with mud. But Mrs. Riley had a pare of horses that made the hole day better for me. I could have watched them gallop shake their manes and prance about all day. Maybe Ill become a farmer someday. Of course, first they'll have to figure out a weigh to get rid of mud!

Use this sentence from *Jack and Jill* by Alcott, and follow the directions in the Lesson Guide.

One smooth path led into the meadow, and here the little folk congregated; one swept across the pond, where skaters were darting about like water-bugs; and the third, from the very top of the steep hill, ended abruptly at a rail fence on the high bank above the road.

Write a simile about skaters:

_____

_____

Use these lines to write your list, and follow the directions in the Lesson Guide.

_____

_____

_____

_____

_____

Use this sentence from *Jack and Jill* by Alcott, and follow the directions in the Lesson Guide.

"Well, no; it usually takes twenty-one days for bones to knit, and young ones make quick work of it," answered the doctor, with a last scientific tuck to the various bandages, which made Jack feel like a hapless chicken trussed for the spit.

Use these lines to write your quotation, and follow the directions in the Lesson Guide.

_____

_____

_____

_____

_____

_____

Did You Know? When quoting something, while commas and periods go inside the quotation marks, colons and semicolons go outside the quotation marks.

What is something other than food that you would describe as delicious?

Literary Example: "Now, however, he was a helpless captive, given over to all sorts of coddling, laziness, and luxury, and there was a droll mixture of mirth and melancholy in his face, as he lay trussed up in bed, watching the comforts which had suddenly robbed his room of its Spartan simplicity. A **delicious** couch was there, with Frank reposing in its depths, half hidden under several folios which he was consulting for a history of the steam-engine, the subject of his next composition." – from *Jack and Jill* by Alcott

Fill in this chart with five nouns, five verbs, five adjectives, and five pronouns from something you are reading.

Nouns	Verbs	Adjectives	Pronouns

Write a short story about what you would do for amusement if you were stuck in bed.

_____

_____

_____

_____

_____

_____

_____

_____

Lesson 106: Spelling

Use the definitions to figure out the word that goes in the blank. Each of them start with the letter a. Alternately someone could read the words for you to spell.

To get up   __ __ __ <u>s</u> __

This describes a verb   __ __ __ __ <u>r</u> __

Acceptance   __ <u>p</u> <u>p</u> __ __ __ __ __

Period of being away   __ <u>b</u> __ __ __ __ __

Very old   __ __ __ __ __ __ <u>t</u>

Good enough   __ __ __ __ <u>u</u> __ __ __

A lawyer   __ __ __ __ __ __ __ <u>y</u>

Go up   __ __ __ __ <u>n</u> __

Exciting experience   __ <u>d</u> __ __ __ __ __ __ __

Favorable position   __ __ __ __ __ __ __ <u>g</u> __

Use these lines to complete the writing assignment from the Lesson Guide.

_____

_____

_____

_____

_____

Write about Christmas day.

_____

_____

_____

_____

_____

_____

_____

_____

_____

Lesson 108: Spelling

How many words can you make out of the following groups of letters? Try to fill each line with a word.

T O L F O H D O

_____   _____

_____   _____

_____   _____

_____   _____

O K R W B O M O

_____   _____

_____   _____

_____   _____

K A A D R B C Y

_____   _____

_____   _____

_____   _____

Lesson 109: Participle Adjectives

Choose the correct adjective to fit the sentence.

The children were _____ by the message.

       inspire   inspired   inspiring

The message was _____ to them.

       inspire   inspired   inspiring

It is _____ to see their reaction.

       inspire   inspired   inspiring

I am _____ by their inspiration.

       inspire   inspired   inspiring

Our vacation was very _____.

       relax   relaxed   relaxing

I felt very _____ on our vacation.

       relax   relaxed   relaxing

Getting a massage is also _____.

       relax   relaxed   relaxing

The _____ tree blocked the road.

       fall   fallen   falling

Don't cry over _____ milk.

       spill   spilled   spilling

Was this lesson _____ to you?

       confuse   confused   confusing

Write an *as/as as/if* sentence following the directions in the Lesson Guide. Then write a short story using that sentence as your first sentence.

_____

_____

_____

_____

_____

_____

_____

_____

_____

Did You Know? The Bible, the most famous book in the world, is full of similes. Probably the best known ones are those used by Jesus Himself, proclaiming, "The Kingdom of Heaven is like..."

Use these lines to write your spelling words from the Lesson Guide. Pay attention to how they are spelled as you write them.

_____   _____

_____   _____

_____   _____

_____   _____

_____   _____

_____   _____

_____   _____

Use these lines to complete the writing assignment from the Lesson Guide.

_____

_____

_____

_____

_____

Lesson 112: Spelling

Use the definitions to figure out the word that goes in the blank. Alternately someone could read the words for you to spell.

A chart of days and weeks   __ __ __ __ __ __ __ __

Line where earth meets sky   __ __ __ __ __ __ __

Top part of a fraction   __ __ __ __ __ __ __ __ __

Contract of insurance   __ __ __ __ __ __

Tool used for cutting   __ __ __ __ __ __ __ __

Tool used for cleaning   __ __ __ __ __ __

Top of a room   __ __ __ __ __ __ __

Maximum that can be held   __ __ __ __ __ __ __ __

Goods or cargo   __ __ __ __ __ __ __

Math   __ __ __ __ __ __ __ __ __

Not a fruit   __ __ __ __ __ __ __ __

A joining together   __ __ __ __ __ __ __ __

Causing great damage   __ __ __ __ __ __ __ __ __ __

Accompanies a driver   __ __ __ __ __ __ __ __

Pain in the head   __ __ __ __ __ __ __ __

Write a short, one-act play. Write the dialogue and describe the action as well.

_____

_____

_____

_____

_____

_____

_____

_____

_____

_____

_____

_____

Lesson 114: Spelling

Find your spelling words along with some extras in the word search below. Words can be found in any direction.

```
M A R R I A G E K L D J F D T F S G K J F G
H V T H W P N I C T O Y E G F K M T B K F J
D I S A S T R O U S L B A C E C G Z I D N N
V H O R I Z O N O L M W J L A T I X V F I U
P F X U P P Q T U U B F B Q Y P M Z E K J M
W E W S Z S H F U L D A M Y R P A S V R K E
Z P Q E N G I C L X T S U H N A G C R C H R
W T O B I T A S M E C L G R G S I H I D M A
H U Y E U V M G G P G D F S P S N E X T F T
B O R A G T S E U J O D U H A E A A G B Y O
P F E C S F V L V C P L Y I D N T D A T O R
R B R W X S L D N P A L I T R G I A V Q J S
Y H Y S U V H N Y O E P N C C E O C C Z J L
S C I S S O R S A T T A Q B Y R N H A G J M
H V A J L W B X A J D I Z H U R E E L Q V V
H S K H L M U R U N A P C D Y H I K E R Z V
S I T E T Y A M E N Z P I E B D O E N T T N
W X S W X P M C U H Q I G X A A R G D D X I
P R A A E U S S P H K I W U Q B X M A W L Y
Z Z H S A E W Q D X P F U B T R L O R T Z P
R H V B D L F W K C E I L I N G F E O I Z X
L K B N A R I T H M E T I C Q B G U P J K Q
```

beautifully	calendar	disastrous	horizon
numerator	passenger	policy	vegetable
vacuum	scissors	headache	marriage
capacity	arithmetic	ceiling	freight

See how many words you can spell correctly now that you've had a few chances to practice. Have someone read them to you.

_____

_____

_____

_____

_____

_____

_____

Use these lines to complete the writing assignment from the Lesson Guide.

_____

_____

_____

_____

_____

Can you spell even more words correctly this time? Have someone read them to you. Learn from any mistakes you make.

_____   _____

_____   _____

_____   _____

_____   _____

_____   _____

_____   _____

_____   _____

Use these lines to complete the writing assignment from the Lesson Guide.

_____

_____

_____

_____

_____

_____

Use these lines to write your spelling words from the Lesson Guide. Pay attention to how they are spelled as you write them.

_____   _____

_____   _____

_____   _____

_____   _____

_____   _____

_____   _____

Use these lines to complete the writing assignment from the Lesson Guide.

_____

_____

_____

_____

_____

Lesson 118: Spelling

Find your spelling words in the word search below. Words are in every direction.

```
R N K M E L R T E P S W Q E F O J Z H W O Z S J C
P K P I T T C F W C U I Q Q P G J Q P W P T I W H
B D I F F I C U L T Y C S U N U A A F Z G E G Q R
X F Y N K F G J Y V T E A H J B O D D Q U K O Z O
W H I N J T Q F R Y F R U O T F Q L R C N W N Z M
G U F M S C D F T S C A X P Z T E W A A N A G K E
U J O L D S X B O H V H E P E D G Q V T W P P W N
V Q W Z T K Q B A L D K J O M G W H Y Y N O N J I
V C G D H Z D E U J I D A S M W P B D U M A T S C
D J U Z U I O T V C S A A I X B L F R H O U C Y I
A A E U Z L D X S P M M G T I H T M S M M K F E D
B F S A O I U P Q U K Q I E C E B T T D U M B S E
C S C G L M M J Q Y O U S U A L L Y X P L Z E A M
R X I W R O Y P I M J L S U N Z C H C K U N B E I
E S C N L Z U P L E B S A R Z E H M M H S Y K R I
T L M V T Z S S E Y Q Y J E I C G A O I E I X C H
S H L A G A R Y Y Q I H E B Z H T Y T H M M E E U
O A R M B T U S Y B E G U I L E D I X H K E N D V
F I B R Q T T N E M A I L R A P V C T O M G M N Q
F G P E F U N U I K B Y J V I E X C S O D E F E S
C U A O A C D E T S E R E T N I Y R N X Y X F Y N
P K G I S U N M A R Y L A N D C B Q J G X Z O D K
E J A L A U G H T E R I G K X J B T Y V V A C Z S
```

chrome	zealous	oxygen	laughter
interested	opposite	decrease	imply
foliage	beguiled	difficulty	archaeologist
cantaloupe	parliament	sensitive	jealousy

Use these lines to complete the writing assignment from the Lesson Guide.

_____

_____

Unscramble the letters below into the correctly spelled word they represent.

E G B E D U L I

_____

Y F I C L I D F U T

_____

O G L F I E A

_____

V E S I T N I E S

_____

P C N E A T A O L U

_____

M A L N A P E R T I

_____

Of the bolded words, circle the one that matches the part of speech to the side of the sentence. Then use the lines for your writing assignment.

Somewhere over the **rainbow, bluebirds** fly.   Preposition

The **painting was displayed above** the tub.   Noun

Her lovely eyes **sparkled under** her glasses.   Adjective

Pick up your **shoes** and put **them in** the bin.   Pronoun

The **normally lively** dog **was acting** mellow.   Adverb

Your mom **will** decide **what** to fix for **dinner**.   Verb

_____

_____

_____

_____

Have someone read you your spelling words as you write them below. Hopefully they're getting easier to spell as you work with them more.

_____   _____

_____   _____

_____   _____

_____   _____

_____   _____

_____   _____

_____   _____

(continued on next page)

Lesson 120: Spelling • Participles

In these sentences, underline the participles and circle the words they modify.

His frown was evidence of his broken spirit.

My sister captivates everyone with her smiling eyes.

The injured bunny fully recovered.

I was awakened early by the singing bird.

In these sentences, underline the participial phrases and circle the words they modify.

Refreshed from her nap, Sarah ran wild.

The shopkeeper, having sold all of his goods, closed his store.

Smiling nervously, Lucas sang his solo.

The children, having been warned, didn't venture out of the yard.

In these sentences, underline the infinitive phrases and circle the words they modify.

Pizza is the best meal to eat.

Jason is the one to ask about photography.

If you'll excuse me, I have a plane to catch.

Your suggestion to read this book was fantastic.

Can you change the listed adjectives into their adverb forms? For instance: The dog was *quick*. He ran *quickly*. If you get stuck, try plugging the words into that sentence and see if you can figure it out. Most of them are easy, but there are a few tricky ones! Use the lines at the bottom for your writing assignment.

jealous	anxious
angry	curious
bold	zealous
sad	good
fast	generous
happy	responsible
hot	hurtful

Write your sentence following the directions in the Lesson Guide. Then use it as the first sentence in a short story.

_____

_____

_____

_____

_____

_____

_____

_____

_____

Did You Know? A semicolon is the only punctuation mark that can always be replaced by another punctuation mark.

Lesson 123: Writing

Write your hyphenated adjectives, following the directions in the Lesson Guide.

_____

_____

Use your hyphenated adjectives in a short story.

_____

_____

_____

_____

_____

_____

_____

_____

Underline the hyphenated adjective in this paragraph from *Jack and Jill* by Alcott. Circle the other hyphen.

A thousand things came up as they sewed together in the afternoon, and the eager minds received much general information in an easy and well-ordered way. Physiology was one of the favorite studies, and Mrs. Hammond often came in to give them a little lecture, teaching them to understand the wonders of their own systems, and how to keep them in order— a lesson of far more importance just then than Greek or Latin, for girls are the future mothers, nurses, teachers, of the race, and should feel how much depends on them. Merry could not resist the attractions of the friendly circle, and soon persuaded her mother to let her do as they did; so she got more exercise and less study, which was just what the delicate girl needed.

Write a sentence that uses a hyphenated adjective, a regular hyphen, and a semicolon.

_____

_____

_____

_____

Answer the questions below to see how well you remember some of the things we've learned during this course.

Which of these is an example of a participle adjective?

- ⭕ snowy
- ⭕ extra-cold snow
- ⭕ fallen snow

Bear and bare are examples of...

- ⭕ homonyms
- ⭕ antonyms
- ⭕ synonyms

Which is a compound sentence?

- ⭕ Since I didn't go to bed on time, I'm really tired.
- ⭕ I need to go to bed, or I'll be really tired tomorrow.
- ⭕ I need to go to bed now!

When I get up in the morning is a (an)...

- ⭕ dependent clause
- ⭕ independent clause

Which is a complex sentence?

- ⭕ I need to get on my pjs, brush my teeth, say goodnight, and get into bed.
- ⭕ I need to go to bed, or I'll be really tired tomorrow.
- ⭕ When I get up in the morning, I'm going to be really tired.

"The snow was a blanket on the lawn" is an example of...

- ⭕ alliteration
- ⭕ a metaphor
- ⭕ a simile

"The skaters darted out like water bugs" is an example of...

- ⭕ alliteration
- ⭕ a metaphor
- ⭕ a simile

(continued on next page)

How many pronouns are in this sentence? They think they can do it all themselves.

- ◯ 5
- ◯ 4
- ◯ 3

Which of these words has a prefix?

- ◯ unprepared
- ◯ notorious
- ◯ creative

Where should the main idea or thesis be stated in an essay's introductory paragraph?

- ◯ in every sentence
- ◯ in the last sentence
- ◯ in the first sentence

Which of these is correct?

- ◯ "I need you now!" He said.
- ◯ "I need you now!" he said.
- ◯ "I need you now." he said.

Which word in this sentence is an adverb? It was rather hot when I went in for the early show.

- ◯ early
- ◯ rather
- ◯ in

A compound sentence is made up of…

- ◯ two independent clauses
- ◯ two dependent clauses
- ◯ an independent clause and a dependent clause

I would like eggs for breakfast is an example of a (an)…

- ◯ dependent clause
- ◯ independent clause

Use this page to brainstorm your fiction piece.

Title: _____

Characters:_____

_____

_____

_____

Beginning:_____

_____

_____

Middle:_____

_____

_____

End:_____

_____

_____

Lesson 141: Common Verb Mistakes

These verbs are commonly misused. Try to match the verb with its definition. Learn from any mistakes you make.

rise _____ A. past tense of lay

raised _____ B. past tense of lie

have raised _____ C. to get up

rose _____ D. rest in an upright position

lie _____ E. past tense of sit

lay _____ F. past participle of raise

laid _____ G. rest in a reclining position

set _____ H. past tense of raise

sat _____ I. put or place something

sit _____ J. past tense of rise

See if you can figure out the right time to use lay and the right time to use lie.

My dog is _____ by the door.
  ○ laying   ○ lying

He often _____ here.
  ○ lays   ○ lies

He has _____ here many times.
  ○ laid   ○ lain

He _____ here just this morning.
  ○ laid   ○ lay

Birds _____ eggs.
  ○ lay   ○ lie

A hen _____ over 200 eggs a year.
  ○ lays   ○ lies

I _____ my toothbrush on the sink.
  ○ lay   ○ laid

The US _____ to the south of Canada.
  ○ lies   ○ lays

Lesson 142: Commonly Confused Words Language Arts 6

Choose whether the missing word should be good or well. Remember that good is an adjective and well is an adverb.

Joy is a _____ artist.
- ○ good   ○ well

She can draw _____.
- ○ good   ○ well

She's also a _____ student.
- ○ good   ○ well

And she reads _____, too.
- ○ good   ○ well

Choose whether the missing word should be your or you're. Remember that your is possessive and you're is a contraction.

_____ book is on the table.
- ○ Your   ○ You're

_____ going to need to move it.
- ○ Your   ○ You're

I think _____ stalling.
- ○ your   ○ you're

_____ dinner will have to wait.
- ○ Your   ○ You're

Choose which word best fits the blank. Learn from any mistakes.

Let's _____ a new attitude.
- ○ adopt   ○ adapt

I can _____ to this environment.
- ○ adopt   ○ adapt

The magician used an _____.
- ○ illusion   ○ allusion

He made an _____ to Shakespeare.
- ○ illusion   ○ allusion

The web_____ was informative.
- ○ site   ○ sight   ○ cite

Please _____ your sources.
- ○ site   ○ sight   ○ cite

You are a _____ for sore eyes.
- ○ site   ○ sight   ○ cite

The sunset was quite a _____.
- ○ site   ○ sight   ○ cite

Lesson 143: Commonly Misused Words

Choose whether the missing word should be affect or effect.

The _____ of thoroughly studying was passing the test.
○ affect   ○ effect

This music positively _____ my mood.
○ affects   ○ effects

The list of side _____ for that drug took the whole commercial break.
○ affects   ○ effects

That documentary deeply _____ me.
○ affected   ○ effected

Choose whether the missing word should be its or it's. Remember that its is possessive and it's is a contraction.

The dog chewed _____ bone.   _____ beginning to rain.
○ its   ○ it's   ○ Its   ○ It's

I think _____ a lovely flower.   The tree still has all _____ leaves.
○ its   ○ it's   ○ its   ○ it's

Choose whether the missing word should be can or may.

_____ I have a snack?   I _____ do a back flip.
○ Can   ○ May   ○ can   ○ may

I _____ see the mall from here.   I _____ decide to join you.
○ can   ○ may   ○ can   ○ may

Lesson 144: Dependent Clauses

Choose which part of the following sentences is the dependent clause.

When we left home yesterday, I forgot to bring my toothbrush.

- ○ when we left home yesterday
- ○ I forgot to bring my toothbrush

Maybe we can find a store when we get to our destination.

- ○ maybe we can find a store
- ○ when we get to our destination

If I don't get a chance to brush them, my teeth start to feel fuzzy.

- ○ if I don't get a chance to brush them
- ○ my teeth start to feel fuzzy

If I can't get a toothbrush, I'll have to find some minty gum.

- ○ if I can't get a toothbrush
- ○ I'll have to find some minty gum

Can you figure out a way to combine the group of sentences into one sentence without losing any of the information?

Fremont is the busiest street in town.
It cuts right through the downtown area.

_____

_____

The leaves are falling off the trees.
The falling leaves temporarily obstruct my view when I'm driving.

_____

_____

Lesson 145: Sentence Fragments

Answer the following questions.

Find the fragment.
- ○ I have so many chores to finish today.
- ○ The vacuuming, sweeping, washing, and drying.
- ○ I should get moving!

Find the fragment.
- ○ My sister has chores.
- ○ Although my sister has chores.
- ○ However, my sister has chores.

Find the fragment.
- ○ My sister and I could work together on our chores.
- ○ My sister and I could work together. On our chores.
- ○ On our chores, my sister and I could work together.

What is true of the following?

When we got our chores done.
- ○ It is a sentence fragment.
- ○ It is a simple sentence.
- ○ It is a compound sentence.
- ○ It is a complex sentence.

What is true of the following?

We got our chores done.
- ○ It is a sentence fragment.
- ○ It is a simple sentence.
- ○ It is a compound sentence.
- ○ It is a complex sentence.

Underline the part of each paragraph that is a fragment.

I went for a jog yesterday afternoon. As I turned the corner, I stumbled face first into a large mud puddle. I stood up and looked around, completely embarrassed. As mud and water dripped down my face and clothes. I decided jogging wasn't for me.

Sylvia went to the mall food court for lunch with her friends. The vast choices overwhelmed her. Japanese, Chinese, subs, pizza, chicken, burgers and fries. It took her longer to decide what she wanted to eat than it did to finish her meal.

Clothes shopping was not fun for Peter. He just didn't care what he wore, as long as he was dressed. Some of his friends were more particular. For instance, Christopher's plaid shirts or Logan's stripes. Peter wasn't particular enough to enjoy shopping for clothes.

Beth was helping her mom with some baking. It smelled like something was burning. Beth opened the oven. Which caused her glasses to fog up with steam. Her mom chuckled and scooped up the fallen, burning chocolate chip and dumped it in the trash.

Lesson 147: Word Builder

Language Arts 6

Choose a piece from each box to build a word that fits the blank in the sentence.

dis	cal
hor	bea
jeal	sep
sen	not

i	ous
ara	ice
si	en
utif	as

tely	able
tive	y
trous	ully
dar	zon

The tear in your skirt is hardly _____.

I could sense her _____ as I described my new, adorable puppy.

The sun is setting beyond the _____.

My eyes are so _____ to light that I need prescription sunglasses.

The missing screw had _____ consequences.

I forgot to turn the _____ to the new month, so my days are all off.

The song was _____ performed.

I think we should drive _____ so we have two cars there.

Lesson 148: Sentence Fragments

Underline the part of each paragraph that is a fragment.

It takes forever to get ready for bed. For some reason, I'm so distractible while I'm trying to do everything. Brushing my teeth, changing my clothes, washing my face, saying my prayers. It's easy to let my mind wander and slow me down.

My favorite game is one where you get to be the mayor of your own city. But it's not all sunshine and roses. You have to make sure there are pipes running water to the city. And lines running electricity. When things aren't going well, your whole city is mad at you. But when things are great, they sing your praises.

On the way to musical rehearsal, we got a flat tire. We have roadside assistance, but they said it would be an hour before they could come. We opted to walk. It was a beautiful day. Good thing!

Jessica's bedroom is a mess. Piles of dirty clothes, clean clothes, dirty dishes, and toys. The crazy thing is that it was just cleaned yesterday. She'll have to clean it again tomorrow. It's bedtime now.

Lesson 149: Writing

Use this page to write your paragraph.

_____

_____

_____

_____

_____

_____

_____

Either write a short story that doesn't use any fragments, or write a poem that only uses fragments.

_____

_____

_____

_____

_____

_____

_____

_____

_____

_____

Use this page to write your paragraph.

_____

_____

_____

_____

_____

_____

_____

Lesson 152: Commas

For each blank in the sentences below, fill in a comma if a comma belongs. Fill in an x if a comma doesn't belong.

Charise wants to be a librarian___ when she grows up___ so in addition to studying literature___ and reading as much as she can___ she also helps sort___ stack___ and put away the books___ at her local library.

"Hey Brian___" ___ I called to my brother.___ "Do you know where we left the football___ when we were done playing with it last week?" Brian answered___ that he couldn't remember where he had put it.

On the way___ to the store___ my mom saw an albino deer running through the trees___ so she opted to skip the store___ to attempt to get its picture.

One dark___ stormy night___ my sisters and I were huddled in the basement. Suddenly___ our brothers jumped out from behind the couch___ startling us all.

Having read and loved all of the author's books___ I was greatly looking forward to her book release___ the following day.

Fill in the missing punctuation in the sentences below.

What was your answer asked Tricia   about going dinner tonight

When we drove through Texas   we visited the following cities   El Paso San Antonio and Houston

The cute as a button baby made cooing noises.

Before you leave for the store make sure that you have the grocery list

I think stuttered Jen that I need to take a break

Fill in any missing apostrophes in the sentences below.

Sarah, Jenny, and Lisa all made the girls soccer team.

Sarah and Jenny remembered their shin guards, but Lisas were left at home.

Without shin guards, she couldnt take part in the scrimmage at practice.

She didnt forget them on game day, though!

She brought hers and a spare for anyone else who might have forgotten theirs.

Lesson 154: Parts of Speech

Of the bolded words, underline the one that matches the part of speech to the side of the sentence.

It's a special treat **to** get **to** eat **in** my bed.   Preposition

Let's **go** for a **run first** thing **in** the morning.   Noun

That **was** such a **relaxing vacation** to Maui.   Adjective

We are **headed to** the park **after** lunch.   Pronoun

The ***Very Hungry*** Caterpillar is a **great book**.   Adverb

The **dance** at the Rec Center **was** a **lot** of **fun**.   Verb

Circle the part of speech that correctly labels the underlined word in each sentence.

It's pouring down <u>rain</u> outside!   noun   adverb   adjective

Did you ask <u>them</u> to join us?   noun   pronoun   adverb

Look at that deer <u>over</u> there!   verb   preposition   noun

The <u>fascinating</u> story captivated me.   noun   verb   adjective

We <u>had</u> a great trip to the fair.   adverb   verb   preposition

Will you be here <u>soon</u>?   noun   adverb   pronoun

Fill in your topic, your thesis statement, and your three points of discussion.

Topic: _____

Thesis statement: _____

_____

_____

_____

Point 1: _____

_____

Point 2: _____

_____

Point 3: _____

_____

Read through your essay and fix any weak spots. Here is your editing checklist again. Remember to aim for a check mark in each box.

Introduction
☐ My introduction begins with an attention grabber.
☐ My introduction has at least three sentences.
☐ My introduction ends with the main idea of my essay.

Body
☐ The body of my essay has at least three paragraphs.
☐ Each paragraph of the body starts with a topic sentence.
☐ Each paragraph of the body has at least three supporting sentences.
☐ Each paragraph of the body has a conclusion sentence.

Conclusion
☐ My conclusion has at least three sentences.
☐ My conclusion restates my main idea.
☐ My conclusion answers the question, "So what?"

Unity
☐ My essay flows well and makes sense.
☐ My essay uses transition words.
☐ My essay is interesting.

Subject Matter
☐ My essay has different sentences – short, long, compound, complex.
☐ My essay uses descriptive words.
☐ All parts of my essay support my main idea.

Grammar/Mechanics
☐ All words are spelled correctly.
☐ There are no grammatical mistakes.
☐ There are no punctuation errors.
☐ There are no fragments.
☐ There are no run-on sentences.

Lesson 163: Appositives

Each sentence contains an appositive. Select the correctly punctuated option from the list of choices.

The scariest animal I've ever seen was in our yard a rabid coyote.
- ◯ The scariest animal I've ever seen, was in our yard, a rabid coyote.
- ◯ The scariest animal I've ever seen was in our yard, a rabid coyote.
- ◯ The scariest animal, I've ever seen, was in our yard a rabid coyote.

My birthday a week from Thursday will be a busy day.
- ◯ My birthday, a week from Thursday, will be a busy day.
- ◯ My birthday, a week from Thursday will be, a busy day.
- ◯ My birthday, a week from Thursday will be a busy day.

The star of the show Julie Andrews has a beautiful voice.
- ◯ The star of the show Julie Andrews, has a beautiful voice.
- ◯ The star, of the show, Julie Andrews has a beautiful voice.
- ◯ The star of the show, Julie Andrews, has a beautiful voice.

Jason is our best quarterback the boy wearing number 12.
- ◯ Jason is our best quarterback, the boy wearing number 12.
- ◯ Jason, is our best quarterback, the boy wearing number 12.
- ◯ Jason is our best quarterback the boy, wearing number 12.

My favorite activities singing and dancing have a time and a place.
- ◯ My favorite activities singing and dancing have a time, and a place.
- ◯ My favorite activities singing, and dancing have a time, and a place.
- ◯ My favorite activities, singing and dancing, have a time and a place.

My friend Angie likes to read.
- ◯ My friend, Angie likes to read.
- ◯ My friend Angie likes to read.
- ◯ My friend, Angie, likes to read.

Fill in the past tense form of the verb given in parentheses.

(wind) If you _____ your watch, why did it stop?

(drive) We _____ to Sacramento in one night.

(kneel) My dad _____ beside me as I prayed.

(ring) The phone _____ four times before stopping.

(grow) The little seed _____ into a huge bush.

Identify the appositives in the following sentences.

My sister Emily has a lot of shoes.
- ○ My
- ○ Sister
- ○ Emily
- ○ Shoes

The word "shoes" makes me think of blisters and trapped toes.
- ○ The word
- ○ shoes
- ○ makes
- ○ trapped

I, the queen of comfort, would be barefoot all the time if I could be.
- ○ I
- ○ the queen of comfort
- ○ all the time
- ○ if I could be

Lesson 165: Commas • Combining Sentences   Language Arts 6

Fill in any missing commas in the sentences below.

The threat of impending storms causes me undue stress.

At face value your idea seems to have merit.

I asked you to pick up milk not eggs.

Bring your pennies nickels and dimes to the fundraiser tomorrow.

My cousin a soccer player likes to run for fun.

Combine the following sentences into a single sentence that contains only one independent clause.

My grandparents live in a simple farm house.
It's on Shadowfax Drive in Gentryville.
They are neighbors of the mayor.

_____

_____

_____

Their yard has a large apple tree.
The branches of the apple tree hold a fantastic rope swing.
We jump from the swing into the creek behind the tree.

_____

_____

_____

Lesson 167: Final Project

Use this sheet to record your resources, or the places where you find information for your final project. The info lines are short on purpose. Don't try to copy a full sentence. Take notes like "made in 1902" or "born on July 6." This will help you not copy what others wrote. Record the titles, authors, and dates of publication.

Topic:_____

Resource 1:_____

Info:_____   Info:_____

Info:_____   Info:_____

Info:_____   Info:_____

Resource 2:_____

Info:_____   Info:_____

Info:_____   Info:_____

Info:_____   Info:_____

Resource 3:_____

Info:_____   Info:_____

Info:_____   Info:_____

Info:_____   Info:_____

Lesson 168: Final Project

Continue to gather your research. Use this sheet to record your resources and notes for your project. Remember that the info lines are short on purpose. Just take notes instead of copying full sentences. This will ensure your work is your own and not copied from someone else.

Resource 4:_____

Info:_____   Info:_____

Info:_____   Info:_____

Info:_____   Info:_____

Resource 5:_____

Info:_____   Info:_____

Info:_____   Info:_____

Info:_____   Info:_____

Resource 6:_____

Info:_____   Info:_____

Info:_____   Info:_____

Info:_____   Info:_____

This is your last lesson for researching and gathering facts. Look for any missing pieces you feel you have and jot your notes below.

Resource 7:_____

Info:_____   Info:_____

Info:_____   Info:_____

Info:_____   Info:_____

Resource 8:_____

Info:_____   Info:_____

Info:_____   Info:_____

Info:_____   Info:_____

Resource 9:_____

Info:_____   Info:_____

Info:_____   Info:_____

Info:_____   Info:_____

Lesson 171: Writing - Essay

Use this page to organize your facts into groups by color. Write the fact on the line and use the box beside the line to label it with the color. Then decide on the order for your facts. Use the first box to number them.

Today you are going to take your topics and write an outline for the body of your report. Each capital letter should be a topic of a paragraph. Aim for *at least* five topics. Each lower case letter is a fact for that topic. If you have more than three facts for a topic, think about how you can divide the topic into two mini topics.

A. _____

    1. _____

    2. _____

    3. _____

    4. _____

B. _____

    1. _____

    2. _____

    3. _____

    4. _____

C. _____

    1. _____

    2. _____

    3. _____

    4. _____

(continued on next page)

D. _____

    1. _____

    2. _____

    3. _____

    4. _____

E. _____

    1. _____

    2. _____

    3. _____

    4. _____

F. _____

    1. _____

    2. _____

    3. _____

    4. _____

(continued on next page)

G. _____

    1. _____

    2. _____

    3. _____

    4. _____

H. _____

    1. _____

    2. _____

    3. _____

    4. _____

I. _____

    1. _____

    2. _____

    3. _____

    4. _____

Lesson 177: Editing Checklist

Read through your research project and fix any weak spots. Here is your editing checklist again. Remember to aim for a check mark in each box.

Introduction
- [ ] My introduction begins with an attention grabber.
- [ ] My introduction has at least three sentences.
- [ ] My introduction ends with the main idea of my project.

Body
- [ ] The body of my essay has at least five paragraphs.
- [ ] Each paragraph of the body starts with a topic sentence.
- [ ] Each paragraph of the body has at least three supporting sentences.
- [ ] Each paragraph of the body has a conclusion sentence.

Conclusion
- [ ] My conclusion has at least three sentences.
- [ ] My conclusion restates my main idea.
- [ ] My conclusion answers the question, "So what?"

Unity
- [ ] My project flows well and makes sense.
- [ ] My project uses transition words.
- [ ] My project is interesting.

Subject Matter
- [ ] My project has different sentences – short, long, compound, complex.
- [ ] My project uses descriptive words.
- [ ] All parts of my project support my main idea.

Grammar/Mechanics
- [ ] All words are spelled correctly.
- [ ] There are no grammatical mistakes.
- [ ] There are no punctuation errors.
- [ ] There are no fragments.
- [ ] There are no run-on sentences.

Lesson 180: Feedback

Read your research project to or with your family. Let them leave feedback for you here.

I liked the report because:_____

_____

Something I learned was:_____

_____

I liked the report because:_____

_____

Something I learned was:_____

_____

I liked the report because:_____

_____

Something I learned was:_____

_____

Congratulations!

You have finished Language Arts 6!

The Easy Peasy All-in-One Homeschool is a free, complete online homeschool curriculum. There are 180 days of ready-to-go assignments for every level and every subject. It's created for your children to work as independently as you want them to. Preschool through high school is available as well as courses ranging from English, math, science, and history to art, music, computer, thinking, physical education, and health. A daily Bible lesson is offered as well. The mission of Easy Peasy is to enable those to homeschool who otherwise thought they couldn't.

The Genesis Curriculum takes the Bible and turns it into lessons for your homeschool. Daily lessons include Bible reading, memory verse, spelling, handwriting, vocabulary, grammar, Biblical language, science, social studies, writing, and thinking through discussion questions.

The Genesis Curriculum uses a complete book of the Bible for one full year. The curriculum is being made using both Old and New Testament books. Find us online at genesiscurriculum.com to read about the latest developments in this expanding curriculum.

Made in the USA
Monee, IL
16 July 2023

39189098R00090